When I Were a Lad...

Snapshots from a time that Health and Safety forgot

Andrew Davies

PORTICO

We Had It Tough...

When I were a lad it were sink or swim. If you couldn't swim after two lengths of pier with Uncle Stan, then they chucked you over the weir and said, "get on with it".

There were none of your fancy Alton Towers thrill rides, neither. For a farthing you could get conductor to swing you round back of tram by your jumper for half a mile...

We didn't have 'Nemesis Revenge',
we had not-letting-go-of-the-kite.

When Mrs Ollerenshawe took us on a tour of the Dales we had a great time...until she started doing handbrake turns.

Footer Were Tough

In our day, footer boots were made for clogging, not dribbling. The aim was to give ball a right good clog. And the golden rule was the shortest lad had to be goalkeeper.

We played every night in our street.
In them days footballs were made out of rhino hide
and weighed as much as a pram. If you tried to
head it, you woke up in hospital.

Youngsters today think they invented footer, but we were well ahead of them. Mr Timms taught us shooting, Mr Arkwright taught us clogging and Mrs Heptinstall taught us the biodynamics of the long throw.

And there were no need to get to match
early. You could stand at back of Barnsley
home game and say,
"Can I go down front, Mister?"

Pets Were Rubbish

After Second World War there were
international shortage of pets. Most of 'em
were eaten. We had to make do with a pet
chicken for three years. Mind you, it did
this amazing trick with a hoop...

If you found a pet, you had to hold onto
it f' dear life.

There were such a shortage, posh kids were
forced to have working-class pets.

...and any old manky cat would do.
Even evil-looking ones that could read
your thoughts.

Me dad brought home an "Abyssinian Terrier" for our sis. She were well chuffed...

...till everyone at school told her it were fox.

The thing that made us really mad
back then were the pet touts.
Yeah, you could have a cat...
if you had the brass.

In our day there were no such thing as supply teachers. If school were short they'd get donkeys in.

If you were lucky, you got
one-to-one tuition.

Fun With Endangered Species

You didn't have to worry about animal civil rights back then. If you wanted to have a panda take your picture, then it were fine.

...and if you were short of a goalie, y'didn't
have to call the World Wildlife Fund to check
if it were okay...

...or ask them if he could help with washing.

You could endanger your own species.
If you ran out of air-rifle targets, next door's
kittens would do. Paper targets with bullseyes
were okay, but they never went "Miaoow!"
when you hit 'em.

Muckin' About

In them days, folk let you get on with stuff.
If you wanted to fall off the edge of
Empire State Building while playing the
Milky Bar Kid, that were fine.

Protective goggles, protective gloves.
What were they all about?

Nobody had seen the film
'Don't Look Now'.

We hardly ever came back from trips
to the zoo with all our classmates...

And if it were stormy, we'd be straight off
to Filey or Scarborough to see if we could
get rid of Cousin Eric.

Frankly, I'm amazed we won the war, our mines were rubbish. You could jump on 'em all afternoon and not even a "tick-tick-tick".

Life were simpler back then. If you wanted to play Humpty Dumpty, no-one was going to stop you.

Everybody looked on the bright side.
They didn't expect things to go wrong.

...except that time at Bridlington when the
escaped alligator weren't actually dead.

And if we overstepped the mark, we knew we'd
get a bit more than a visit to the "naughty step".
A couple of hours in waste paper bin soon taught
you all you needed to know about toeing the line.

First published in the United Kingdom in 2011 by
Portico Books
10 Southcombe Street
London
W14 0RA

An imprint of Anova Books Company Ltd
Copyright © Anova Books 2010

This edition published in 2011 for Index Books Ltd.

ISBN 13: 978-1-907554-50-6

A CIP catalogue record for this book is available from
the British Library.

11 10 9 8 7 6 5 4 3 2 1

Reproduction by Rival Colour Ltd.
Printed by 1010 Printing International Ltd., China.

All pictures courtesy of Corbis with the exception of:
Pages 3, 11, 13, 17, 27, 41, 43, 53, 55, 57, courtesy
of Getty Images.

Picture selection committee: Joanna Heygate, Dicken
Goodwin, Frank Hopkinson.